Coloring book for adults and kids amazing sharks image for design

This coloring book
is belongs to

____

____

____

Sea Animals

1.Jellyfish 2.Globefish 3.Crab
4.Shrimp 5.Starfish 6.Fish 7.Octopus
8.Shark 9.Whale 10.Seahorse

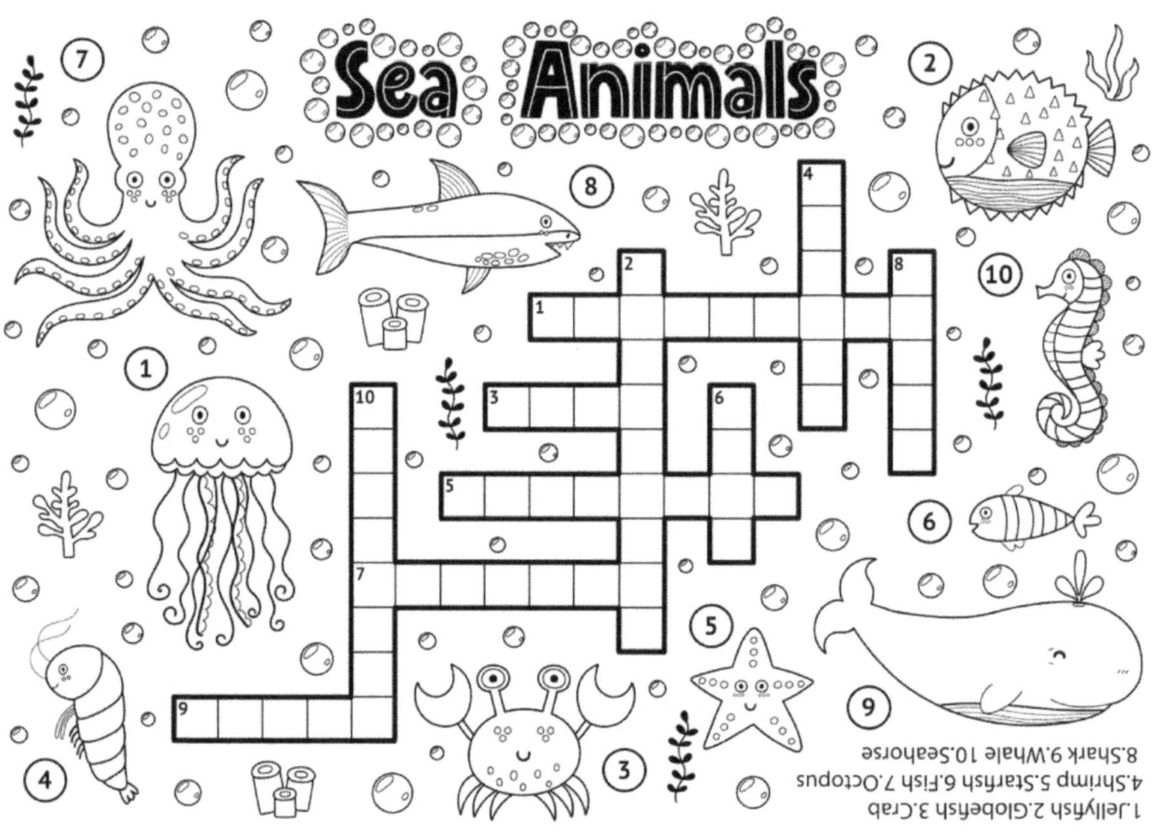

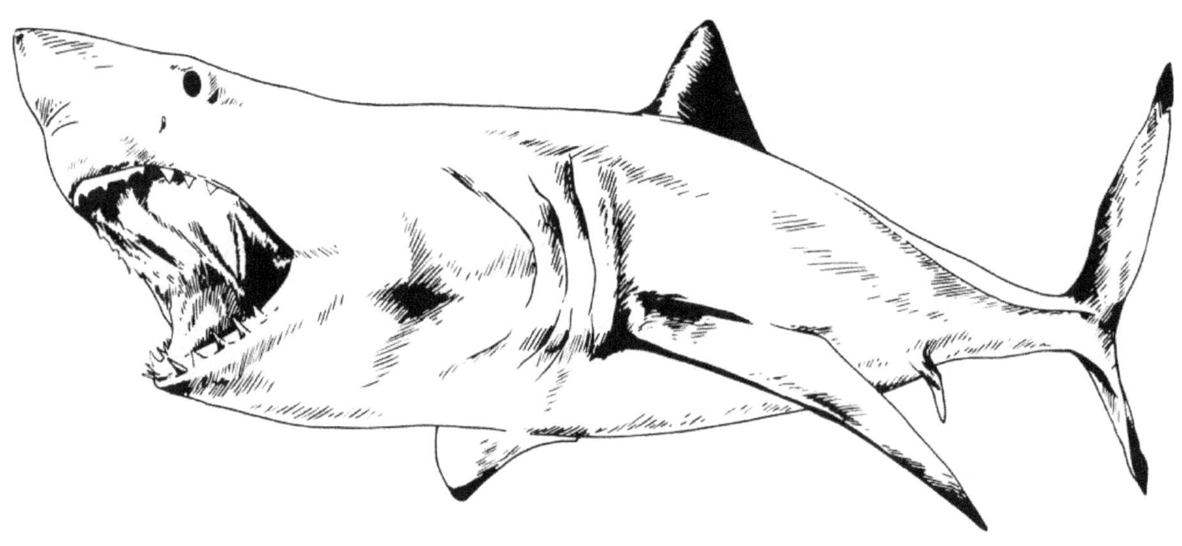

Make a wave

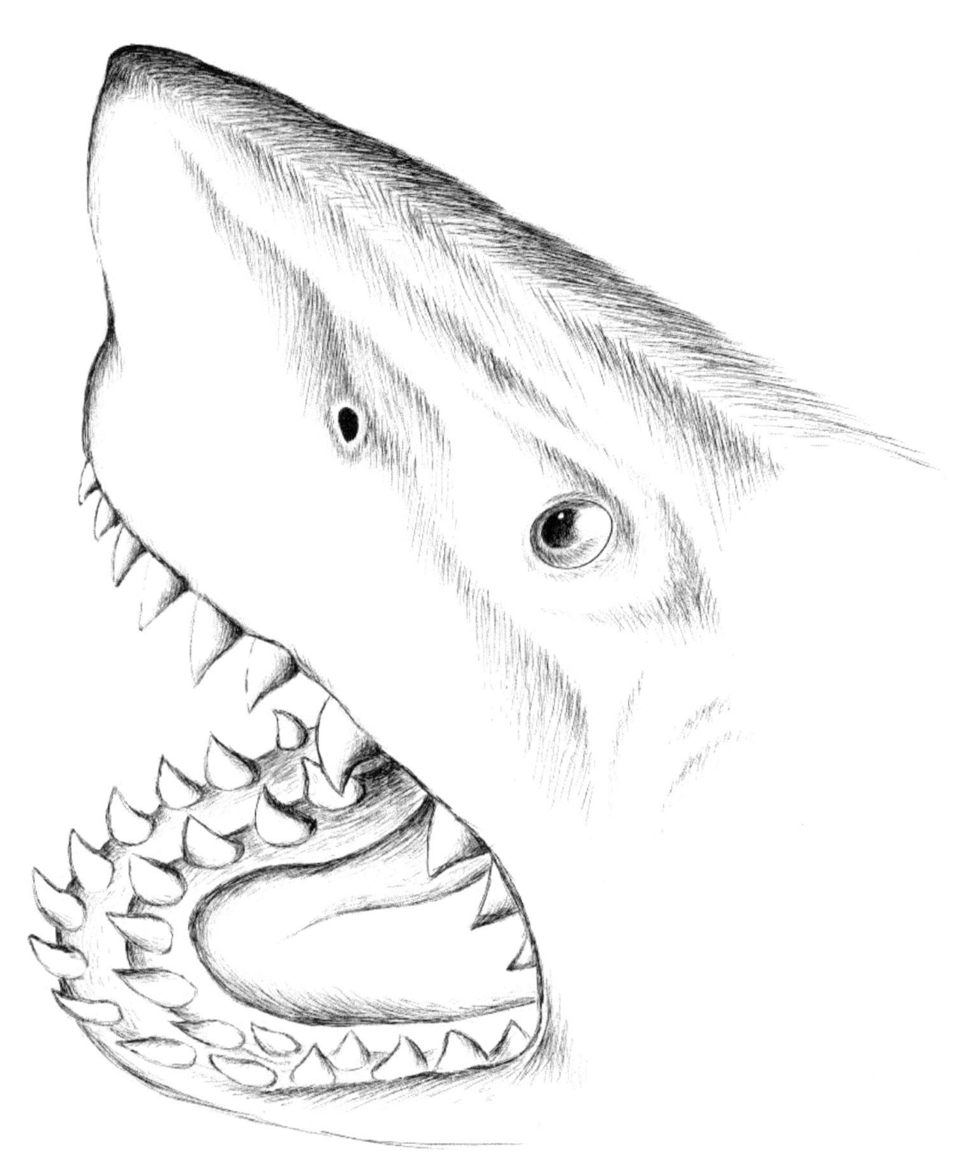

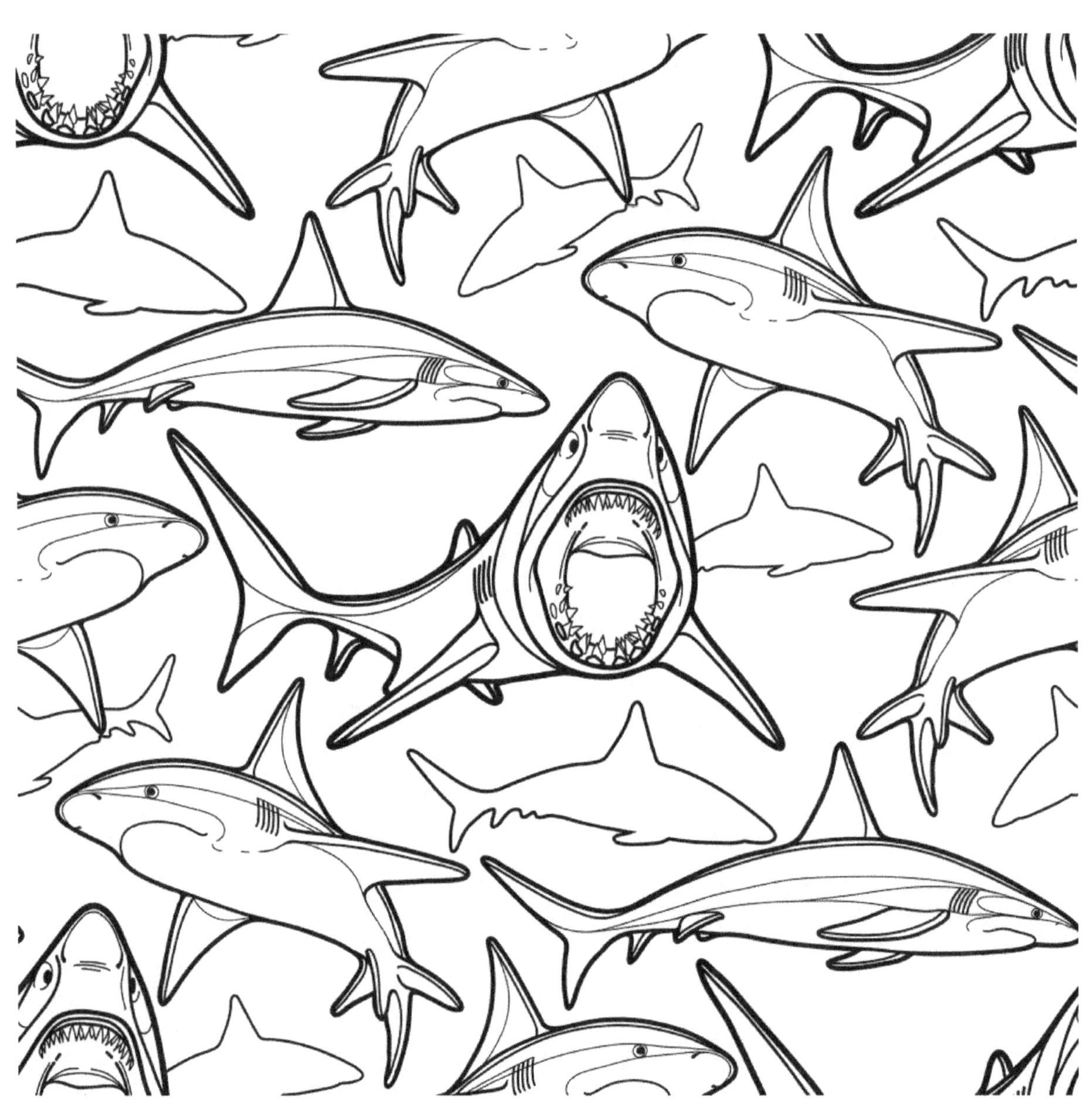

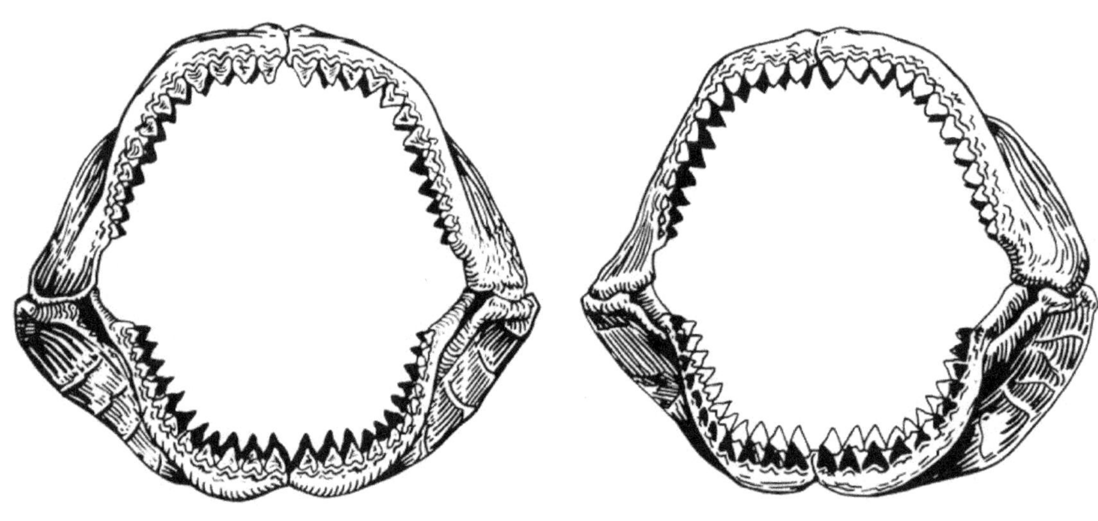

www.ingramcontent.com/pod-product-compliance
Lightning Source LLC
Chambersburg PA
CBHW080038260726
48658CB00007B/2661